The Best Day Ever

Text copyright © 2019 by Micah Brewster
Photographs copyright © 2019 by Diana Ruth Brewster
All rights reserved

Published by J2B Publishing LLC, Pomfret, MD

No part of this book may be reproduced or transmitted in any form or by any means, electronic or mechanical, including photocopying, recording, or by any information storage and retrieval system, without written permission from the publisher. The only exception is brief quotations for reviews.

For information address:
   J2B Publishing LLC
   4251 Columbia Park Road
   Pomfret, MD 20675
   www.J2BLLC.com

ISBN: 978-1-948747-54-7

Visit www.GladToDoIt.net

The Best Day Ever

Micah Brewster

J2B Publishing

One day, the Brewster and Jewell Families went to Legoland. They were all excited. Micah and Judah were especially excited!

They walked into Legoland. It was amazing! The first ride they saw was Lego cars to drive. They ran towards them and hopped in line.

They waited for twenty minutes, but it was worth it! It was like driving a real car. Micah's car was blue. Judah's was blue, also. They rode several times.

They went to a huge model of Lego City, USA. It was a huge set-up of Legos. It had moving cars and boats in real water.

Then they went to a huge Lego water table and built their own boats and raced them down the Lego river.

They walked through Lego land for a while and then saw it, the ride they had all been waiting for. The dragon roller coaster! They rode it ten times. It was the best!

Then they walked through the park a little bit more. They saw an ice cream stand. They asked mom for some ice cream and she said, "Yes!" They both got large mint chip ice cream cones.

At the end of their time at Legoland they went to a building where you could build your own Lego man. That was the best day ever!

The End

Meet the Author

Micah Brewster went to Legoland with his friends, the Jewels, and wrote a story about it when he was nine.

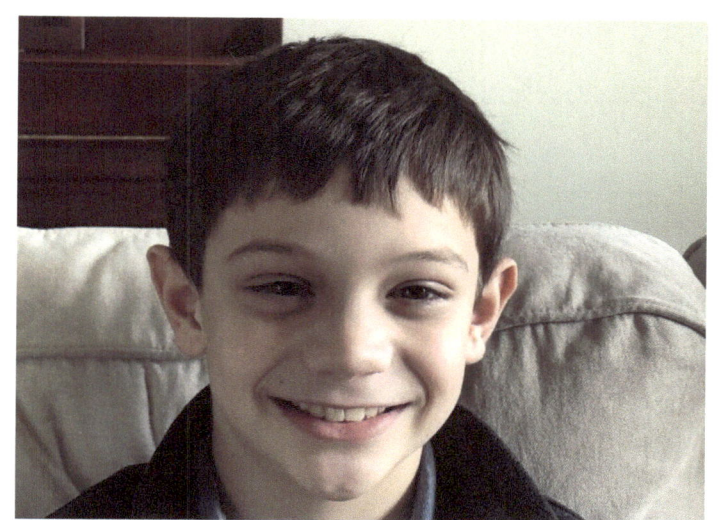

Meet the Photographer

Diana Ruth Brewster is the mother of Micah and 5 other children and loves to photograph them.

Write Your Own Story of a Favorite Trip

Draw a Picture or Paste a Photograph to Go With Your Story

Write Your Own Story of a Favorite Trip

Draw a Picture or Paste a Photograph to Go With Your Story

Write Your Own Story of a Favorite Trip

Draw a Picture or Paste a Photograph to Go With Your Story

Write Your Own Story of a Favorite Trip

Draw a Picture or Paste a Photograph to Go With Your Story

Write Your Own Story of a Favorite Trip

Draw a Picture or Paste a Photograph to Go With Your Story

www.ingramcontent.com/pod-product-compliance
Lightning Source LLC
Chambersburg PA
CBHW042119040426
42449CB00002B/108